Your Environment

Future ENERGY

Sally Morgan

Stargazer Books

How to use this book

This series has been developed for group use in the classroom, as well as for students reading alone. Its text on two levels allows students of mixed reading abilities to enjoy reading and talking about the same topic.

(1) The main text and (2) picture captions give essential information in short, simple sentences. They are set in the © Sassoon font, recommended for maximum legibility. This font style helps students bridge the gap between their reading and writing skills.

(3) Below each picture caption is a subtext that explains the pictures in greater detail, using more complicated sentence structures and vocabulary.

(4) Text backgrounds are cream or a soft yellow to reduce the text/background contrast to support students with visual processing difficulties or other special needs.

Wind energy

Fossil fuels are running (1) out. People are looking for new sources of energy.

Wind power is a very useful source of energy.

⬆ **Wind farms on a hill** (2)

(3)

Wind farms are put in places where there is wind all year. There are many wind farms on the mountains behind Los Angeles. (4)

© Aladdin Books Ltd 2006

Designed and produced by Aladdin Books Ltd

First published in the United States in 2006 by Stargazer Books c/o The Creative Company 123 South Broad Street P.O. Box 227 Mankato, Minnesota 56002

Printed in Malaysia

All rights reserved

Editor:
Jim Pipe

Educational Consultant:
Jackie Holderness

Science Consultant:
Nigel Hawkes

Design:
Flick, Book Design and Graphics
Pete Bennett—PBD

Picture Research:
Brian Hunter Smart

Library of Congress Cataloging-in-Publication Data

Morgan, Sally.
  Future energy / by Sally Morgan.
  p. cm. -- (Your environment)
  ISBN 1-59604-061-0
  1. Power resources--Juvenile literature. 2. Energy conservation--Juvenile literature. I. Title. II. Series.

TJ163.23.M67 2005
333.79--dc22
                    2004058617

CONTENTS

Introduction

All life needs energy. Plants and animals need energy to live and grow.

Energy lights our cities. It warms our homes and cooks our food. Energy powers our machines.

Most of the energy we use comes from coal, oil, and gas. But these fuels are running out. We need to find new sources of energy.

◁ **Your body needs energy to move about.**

We get our energy from the food we eat. Energy is needed for our bodies to grow. We need energy to walk and run.

A person who does a lot of exercise every day needs to eat more food than somebody who sits at a desk all day.

⬇︎ ⬆︎ **What would life be like without energy?**

If the electricity goes off, many things do not work. There would be no lights, heating, TV, or computers.

Take a look around your kitchen. How much is powered by electricity? How could you cook if you had no electricity or gas?

◁ **We can use the sun's energy again and again.**

The sun will provide us with light and heat for five billion years. It is a "renewable" energy source—we can use it again and again. As new trees can be planted, wood is another renewable source. However, fuels such as coal, oil, and gas are not renewable. They take many millions of years to form.

What are fuels?

A fuel is something that can provide energy. Fuels include gasoline for a car, gas for a stove, or wood for a fire.

All fuels store energy. Power plants use the energy stored in fuels to create electricity.

To use a fuel, we transfer its energy. For example, we can only use the energy stored in a chocolate bar when we eat it. We transfer the energy to our body.

▷ **Wood is a biofuel. When it burns, it gives off heat and light.**

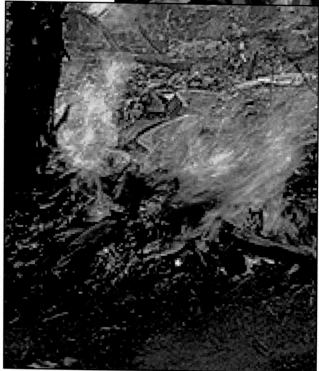

Biofuels are fuels that come from living things. Other biofuels include leaves and dried dung from animals such as cows and sheep.

Like coal and oil, the energy in biofuels came from the sun. This energy was trapped by plants and stored as chemical energy. When a biofuel burns, this stored energy is converted into heat and light.

◁ Oils from plants and animals are fuels.

Plants such as sunflowers and olives have oily seeds and nuts. The oil can be removed and burned as a fuel.

In the past, people also used the fat from cows, sheep, and even whales for candles, lamps, and cooking.

△ Power plants use coal, oil, or gas to make electricity.

Inside a power plant, burning coal or gas releases heat. This heat is used to boil water which produces steam. The steam is used to create, or generate, electricity.

▽ What energy do you use?

We use the chemical energy in food to fuel our bodies. We use electrical energy to power TVs, computers, dishwashers, and microwave ovens.

Every time you travel in a car, airplane, or bus, you use gasoline or electricity. The stored chemical energy in batteries powers our cell phones and cameras. How many types of energy do you use in a single day?

What are fossil fuels?

Fossil fuels are fuels such as oil, gas, and coal. We now depend on fossil fuels to power cars and industry.

These fuels formed from animals and plants that died hundreds of millions of years ago. That is long before the time of the dinosaurs.

Because fossil fuels take so long to form, they are nonrenewable.

⬆ **Digging coal from an open cast mine.**

⬆ **Oil is pumped from below the ground as thick, black crude oil.**

After being pumped from the ground, crude oil is pumped along pipes or carried in huge tankers to a refinery. Here the oil is heated and treated to separate it into different products such as gasoline, diesel, and kerosene.

Coal that lies near the surface is dug from the ground. This creates open cast mines. Deep coal is mined by digging shafts that reach deep into the ground. Miners dig out long underground tunnels.

The coal is carried by train to power plants. Here it is burned to create electricity.

◁ **Natural gas is pumped to our homes along pipes.**

Like oil, natural gas is formed from the remains of tiny plants and microbes that lived in the sea long ago. You cannot see or smell natural gas, so it has to be mixed with a chemical to give it an odor. Then people can smell it if there is a gas leak.

▽ **The world is running out of fossil fuels.**

Nobody is sure how much coal, oil, and gas is left. It is likely that oil and gas will last another 30 to 50 years, while coal may last a couple of hundred years.

It may be possible to get oil from rocks known as oil shale. But this process uses a lot of energy and damages the environment.

9

Other energy sources

Fossil fuels are not our only energy sources. There is nuclear power and power from moving water.

Wood is the main source of energy in many parts of the world. Other renewable sources, such as the wind and sun, are becoming important.

△ **A hydroelectric dam on the river**

△ **Nuclear fuels produce lots of energy—and poisonous waste.**

Nuclear power plants use uranium as a fuel. Uranium is made up of large atoms. When these atoms are split into smaller atoms, huge amounts of energy are released. This is used to make electricity.

However, nuclear power produces radioactive waste, which is poisonous to all living things.

When a dam is built across a river it creates a large lake or reservoir. The water falls through pipes in the dam.

This spins a turbine which generates electricity. The taller the dam, the farther the water falls and the more electricity can be produced.

⬇ **Millions of people use wood for heat or cooking.**

About half of the world's people burn wood for heating and cooking. Trees such as poplar are grown especially for use as fuel.

Wood is a renewable source of energy. However, in some parts of the world, especially Africa, too many people living in the same place use up wood faster than it can be regrown.

⬆ **Wind power is a renewable source of energy.**

There have been windmills in Europe for over 800 years. But countries in Europe are now turning to wind power as a source of energy. By 2008, a quarter of all of Denmark's power will by supplied by wind turbines like the ones above.

Energy problems

When we burn fossil fuels they create gases that dirty the air. Oil spills harm coasts and wildlife.

Coal mines destroy large areas of countryside. Nuclear energy creates dangerous waste.

However, the biggest problem is that fossil fuels are running out.

We need to find other sources of energy—now!

▷ **Oil spills can cover beaches in oil and kill birds.**

Huge oil tankers carry millions of gallons of oil around the world. Accidents can cause oil spills. Now all new tankers have to have two hulls, one inside the other. This means that there is less chance of an oil spill.

⬆ Nuclear waste can remain harmful for thousands of years.

Some people believe that nuclear energy can solve the world's energy problems.

However, scientists have yet to find a safe way of storing the radioactive waste produced by nuclear power plants.

▷ Sea levels may rise as the world gets warmer.

When fossil fuels burn they release the gas carbon dioxide. This is called a greenhouse gas because it traps heat in the earth's atmosphere. As a result, the earth is getting warmer, causing a wide range of environmental problems.

⬇ Why must we find new energy sources?

In 2001, an electrical power crisis in California drew world attention to a shortage of oil and gas. Power cuts all over the world have also been caused by a failed supply of fossil fuels.

Imagine life without electricity or gasoline. That is why governments around the world are looking for new ways to provide energy.

At the same time, we all need to learn how to use much less energy than we do now.

Planning for the future

The world's population is growing. So more energy is needed, just when we are running out of fossil fuels.

In the past, Europe and North America used the most energy.

Now people in countries such as India and China are also using more and more energy.

What can we do?

▷ **People can use renewable energy.**

People may have to make better use of renewable energy sources, such as wind and wave power and solar energy.

These energy sources are unlimited and so will never run out. They produce far less pollution too.

△ **People can use buses, not cars.**

Modern cars use a lot less fuel for the same journey than they did 30 years ago.

However, new technology is only one solution. If more people used mass transit, it would make a big difference to the amount of energy used.

We live in a world where it is easier to throw something away and buy a new one, rather than repair it. People want to own the latest computer or TV. This means that every year millions of TVs and computers are thrown away, even though they still work.

This is a great waste. We should all recycle or reuse more to reduce the demand for raw materials. How much garbage does your family throw out each week?

Cars can use fuels made from crops such as oilseed rape.

Oilseed rape is grown for its oil, which is used in cooking. This oil can also be converted into a biofuel and used in vehicle engines or as heating oil.

Energy crops like rape could be grown more widely to produce a range of fuel oils.

15

More energy from fossil fuels

When a power plant burns coal, it turns only a third of the coal's energy into electricity. The rest is wasted as heat.

Making more efficient power plants will save a lot of energy.

New inventions such as hybrid cars and LED lights can help to save energy, too.

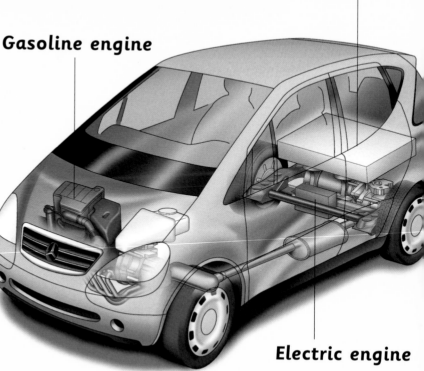

Gasoline engine

Battery pack

Electric engine

▷ **LEDs use less electricity than light bulbs or TV screens.**

A light bulb is powered by electricity. Some of the electrical energy is changed to light, but most is converted to heat.

Almost all the electrical energy in LEDs is turned to light, so less energy is wasted. Many towns are introducing LED traffic lights to save energy. In the next ten years, many homes may have LED lights too.

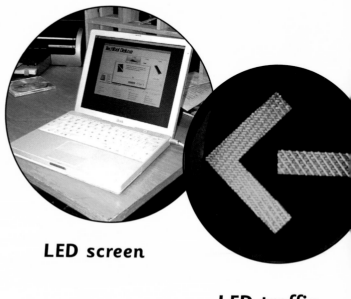

LED screen

LED traffic light

A hybrid car travels over 46 mi (74km) on 1 gallon (4 liters) of fuel.

Half of the world's oil is used to fuel vehicles. So new cars need to travel farther on less fuel. Hybrid cars do this by using an electric motor for slow speed and a gasoline engine at high speed.

A battery stores energy from the gasoline engine. Hybrid engines are clean too—they reduce harmful gas emissions by half.

A heat exchanger uses waste heat to heat water.

As power plants and generators produce electricity, they release lots of waste heat. Heat exchangers use this waste heat to warm up water. This can then be used to heat a home, an office, or a factory.

Big cars are "gas guzzlers."

In 1925, the Model T Ford traveled 19 miles on a gallon (8 km on a liter) of fuel. Eighty years later, some of the latest cars can travel up to 62 mpg (25 kpl). But not all modern cars are so efficient.

People like large cars. These cars require more power to move them, so they need big engines. Large cars of the 1970s were nicknamed "gas guzzlers." They only traveled 8-12 mpg (3-5 kpl). But some of today's big 4-wheel drive cars only travel 15-25 mpg (6-10 kpl).

17

Wind energy

As fossil fuels run out, many countries are looking for new supplies of energy. Wind is one of the most important of these.

Wind turbines have blades that are turned by the wind. The blades are linked to a generator. This creates electricity when it moves.

▷ **Wind pumps pump water from under the ground.**

Wind pumps have been used throughout the world to pump water from below the ground, especially in dry areas.

These pumps can only do one job: pump water. But the electricity from a modern wind turbine can also be used to heat and light several villages.

△ **Groups of turbines are called wind farms.**

Wind farms are put in windy places—there are many wind farms on the mountains behind Los Angeles.

Some wind farms have been built in shallow water a short distance from the coast. These offshore wind farms are less visible, but they can damage the fragile marine environment.

18

◁ Wind turbines turn wind energy to electrical energy.

Turbines with blades are able to generate more electricity. For example, a single 130-ft (40-m) -high wind turbine can generate enough electricity for about 100 to 150 homes.

△ Wind power has been used for hundreds of years.

Wind power has been used to move sailing boats or turn the sails of windmills. A windmill's sails are attached to grinding wheels. When the sails turn, they move the wheels that grind the wheat into flour.

▽ Wind farms are noisy and can harm wildlife.

Wind turbines can only be built in places where it is windy all year round. Even so, there are calm days when the blades do not turn. Wind turbines are noisy too. This can disturb local people.

Wind turbines need deep foundations in the ground, so a large hole has to be dug for each one and then this is filled with concrete. Once the turbines are built, birds may be killed when they fly into the blades.

Water energy

Water is another useful source of renewable energy. We can use the energy in waves, water currents, and in hot water from the ground.

We can use water turbines to change the energy of moving water or steam to electricity.

⬆ **This power plant makes electricity from hot water in the ground.**

⬆ **Water falling over this waterfall has lots of energy.**

Flowing water can turn a wheel that lifts water from a river onto fields of crops. Water mills have a wheel that is turned by the water too.

Hydroelectric power plants use the power of falling water to turn turbines that create electricity. They are often built near dams.

An erupting volcano brings rocks to the surface that are so hot they are liquid. Deep in the ground, these rocks heat water to 660 °F (350°C).

Geothermal power plants use this hot water to create steam that drives a turbine.

20

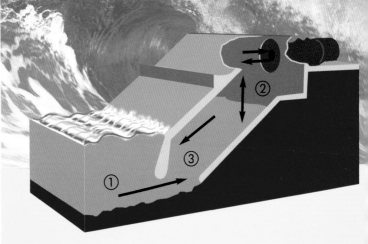

⬆ Wave energy can create electricity too.

Waves have a lot of energy as they crash onto the shore. This energy can be converted to electricity.

There is a wave power plant on Islay, an island off the coast of Scotland. The plant generates electricity for the local villages.

① The waves rush into a sloping chamber built along the shore.

② The waves push air in the chamber against a big turbine, making it spin around. It creates electricity like a wind turbine.

③ When the waves fall back, they suck out of the chamber. This makes the turbine spin too.

⬆ Water turbines use flowing water to create electricity.

Water turbines use the power of the tides to create (generate) electricity. As the water rushes up a river or estuary, the current turns the giant turbines.

A tidal barrage works more like a dam. It traps water, then lets it flow to generate electricity. However, a tidal barrage interferes with the flow of water and can harm wildlife habitats.

Solar energy

The sun supplies the earth with a constant supply of light and heat.

We can use the sun's heat to dry clothes outdoors. Plants use the sun's light to make their own food.

Sunlight can also be used to heat water or make electricity. We call this "solar" power.

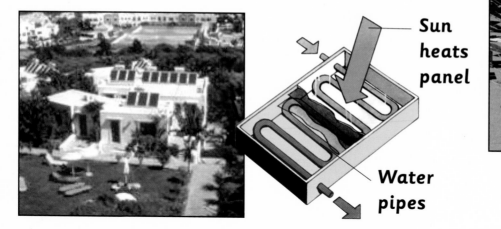

Sun heats panel

Water pipes

⌂ Solar panels on a roof use the sun's heat to create hot water.

Solar panels are usually black metal plates that are attached to water pipes. The plates transfer the sun's heat to water flowing along the pipes. The warm water can be used for washing or heating.

Solar panels work best in sunny places, since when the weather is cloudy, there is no hot water.

◁ Solar cells use the sun's light to power satellites.

Photovoltaic (PV) cells take light energy and turn it into electricity.

Today's PV cells are expensive to make and only ten percent of the light falling on them is converted to electrical energy. However, they are improving all the time.

You may be surprised by the number of uses of photovoltaic cells. Small photovoltaic cells power watches, calculators, and outdoor lights, while more complex systems can supply electricity to satellites in space.

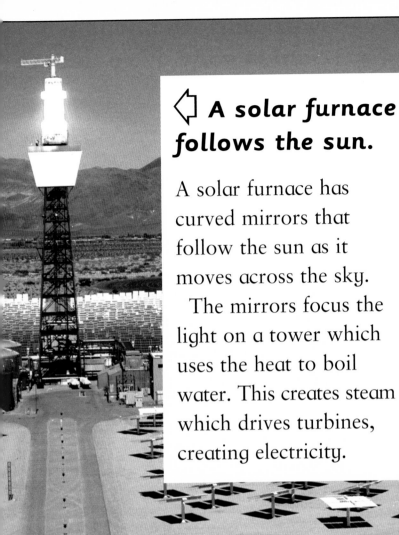

◁ A solar furnace follows the sun.

A solar furnace has curved mirrors that follow the sun as it moves across the sky.

The mirrors focus the light on a tower which uses the heat to boil water. This creates steam which drives turbines, creating electricity.

◁ Solar panels provide power in remote areas.

People in many parts of the world still do not have an electricity supply as they live too far from a power plant.

Solar energy is changing this. It can supply villagers with hot water and electricity for appliances such as refrigerators. It can power small airstrips to help tourism in remote places.

Plant fuels

Solar power is not as cheap as using fossil fuels.

But we can use the sun's energy to grow plant fuels such as sugar cane and soybeans.

Wood is still an important fuel. Trees such as willow and poplar are grown for firewood.

⇧ **This bus runs on oil made from soybeans.**

⇧ **A car fuel called gasohol can be made from sugar cane.**

Sugar cane is grown widely in Brazil. The stems of the sugar cane are cut and the sugar is extracted. The sugar is used to make alcohol. Then the alcohol is mixed with gasoline to make a fuel called gasohol.

Using oils made from plants is not a new idea. The very first diesel engine ran on groundnut oil in 1900.

Many buses in Europe run on oil made from oilseed rape. New diesel engines are being developed that can run on a mixture of plant oil and diesel fuel.

Fast-growing cottonwood trees are grown for fuel.

Trees such as cottonwood and hazel can be cut down to the ground and regrown. Shoots grow from the stump and the stems are harvested every five to ten years. This is called coppicing.

Fast-growing trees such as willow are grown as a crop too.

Trees from this softwood forest are being harvested.

Fast-growing trees such as pine and Douglas fir can be harvested after 30 to 50 years. Once the trees are felled, young trees are planted in their place. This creates plenty of wood for the future.

Buried garbage gives off methane gas. This can be used as fuel.

When living things die and rot, they release a mixture of gases including methane. Methane is produced in landfill sites where garbage is buried in the ground and allowed to rot.

The gas can be used as a fuel. In some places, waste from animals is placed in underground chambers called biogas digesters. The waste releases methane which is used for cooking and heating water.

Fuel cells

A battery stores chemical energy. When you use one, this energy turns to electrical energy until all the chemicals are used up.

Batteries take a lot of energy to make and create harmful waste. So fuel cells may replace batteries.

A fuel cell stores energy using hydrogen gas. The only waste is water so these cells are very clean.

▷ **Hydrogen gas can be made from water.**

Hydrogen gas is made by passing electricity through water. This process is called electrolysis. The hydrogen is collected and used as a fuel.

Hydrogen can also be made from natural gas by a steam reformer. However, both processes require a lot of energy from fossil fuels.

▷ **These cars use hydrogen as a fuel.**

Hydrogen may be the fuel of the future. When hydrogen burns in air, it releases energy that could power a car engine.

If a cheap way of producing hydrogen could be found, it may solve our energy problems.

◁ Fuel cells power this swimming pool.

A fuel cell contains two chemicals that react together to produce electricity. At the moment fuel cells are expensive, very large, and heavy.

However, they will get smaller and cheaper. In the future, every house may have its own fuel cell.

Wasserstoff

Linde

Wasserstoff

Small batteries are used in radios, toys, and remote controls. Some batteries can be used only once and then thrown away. Others can be recharged by passing electricity through them to build up a store of energy.

How many batteries do you use each week? Why is it better to use rechargeable batteries than "one-use" batteries?

Saving energy

Everybody can try to reduce the quantity of energy they use each day. People can ride a bicycle or walk rather than drive.

Homes can be insulated so that heat does not escape.

People can wear more clothes rather than turn the heating up. Lights can be switched off.

▷ **Make use of recycling centers.**

We throw away a lot of garbage and some of it could be reused or recycled. This means using old things to make new things.

Recycling reduces the quantity of raw materials that have to be taken from the ground to make new items, and less energy is needed in their manufacture.

◁ **Trapping heat can save energy.**

One of the biggest bills in many houses is for heating. Many older houses can save energy and money by trapping heat. Insulation stops heat escaping through the roof. Double-glazing reduces the heat that escapes through windows.

◁ There are no cars in this street.

People in developing countries use far less fuel than people in the developed areas of the world. They do not throw as many things away and they recycle more. They also rely more on renewable energy sources such as wood and biogas.

◁ Electric goods have labels that show the energy they use.

Many refrigerators, washing machines, and dishwashers have labels telling people how much electricity they use.

Machines with an "A" rating are energy efficient. This means that they are designed to do their job using as little energy as possible.

⬇ Find out more! One way to save energy is to walk to school.

If you want to find out more about energy, try these useful websites:

- Energy Information Administration www.eia.doe.gov/kids/
- Energy quest www.energyquest.ca.gov
- Future energy www.futureenergies.com
- Green schools around the world www.ase.org/section/program/greenschl
- The Canadian Renewable Energy Network (CanREN) www.canren.gc.ca/school/index.asp

What can you do?

As you have read, most of the world's electricity is made using fossil fuels.

Fossil fuels are running out. However, we can all help by making a saving on the electricity we use. This will help the supplies to last longer.

See how many ways you can save energy in a week.

⬆ 1. Switch off lights!

You can cut down the amount of electricity you use by turning off lights when they are not needed.

⬅ 2. Have a shower rather than a bath.

A five-minute shower uses only two-fifths of the hot water needed for a bath. Also, don't run hot water unless you need it.

⬅ 3. Turn off computers and TVs.

You can make a sticker or a sign to hang next to switches that says "Turn it off" or "Don't Forget!"

4. Walk, cycle, or take the bus.

Today, people jump in their cars to drive just a few minutes. But every time we get in a car we produce pollution, clog up the highways, and use up valuable fossil fuels. So walking, riding a bicycle, or using mass transit makes our environment cleaner, and saves energy.

5. Save energy at school.

In many countries around the world there are "green" or "eco" schools that are finding ways to save energy, by:

• fitting energy-saving light bulbs

• insulating buildings

• buying only energy-efficient machines.

Why not ask your teacher what your school is doing to save energy?

GLOSSARY

Battery—A cell that produces electrical energy from chemicals.

Biogas—A gas produced by rotting vegetation that can be collected and used as a fuel.

Energy—What is needed to make things happen or to do work.

Fossil Fuels—Fuels formed over many millions of years from the remains of dead animals and plants, for example coal and oil.

Fuel—A chemical that releases heat when it burns.

Geothermal—Heat from hot rocks in the ground.

Hydroelectric power—Electricity made from water falling to turn turbines and generators.

Pollution—Unwanted or harmful materials released into the environment, such as the gases released when fossil fuels are burned.

Renewable—Something that can be replaced so it will never run out.

Solar power—Electricity made using heat or light from the sun.

Turbine—A machine that is used to convert movement energy into electrical energy.

INDEX

Photocredits

Abbreviations: l-left, r-right, b-bottom, t-top, c-center, m-middle

Front cover tl, b, back cover tl, 5c, 8ml, 9mr, 10ml, 11ml, 15br, 18bm, 21tr — Comstock. Front cover c, 2mr, 3br, 9br, 12tr, 12br, 13tr, 18-19t, 20ml, 24c, 25tr, 25ml, 28c, 29tr — Photodisc. Front cover tr, 17ml, 26bm, 27bl — Courtesy of The Linde Group. Back cover tr, 1, 22br — Yellowstone National Park/National Park Service. 3tr, 4-5t, 14-15t, 28-29t — Flat Earth. 3mr, 19br — www.europa.eu.int. 4bl, 23mr — Corbis. 5tr, 7br, 16br both, 17br, 27tr all, 28mr, 29bm, 30tr — Jim Pipe. 5br — Digital Vision. 6-7t, 8-9t, 19ml, 22tr — Digital Stock. 6br — Bob Nichols/USDA. 7ml — U.S. Department of Energy. 9ml, 14bm — www.greenhouse.gov.au. 10-11t, 11br, 15ml — Corel. 13tl — www.adelaide.edu.au. 13bm — Photo Essentials. 16tr — www.mercedes-benz.com. 20tr — www.calpine.com. 21tl — Courtesy of Marine Current Turbines Ltd. 22ml, 22-23t — www.wireO.ises.org. 24ml — David Nance/USDA. 24tr — Keith Weller/USDA. 25mt — Peggy Greb/USDA. 26-27t — PBD. 30c — Flick Smith. 30bl, 31 both — Brand X Pictures.